Illustrations
of
The Book of Job

By

William Blake

Illustrations of the Book of Job
Invented and Engraved by William Blake

ISBN-13: 978-1722204044

ISBN-10: 1722204044

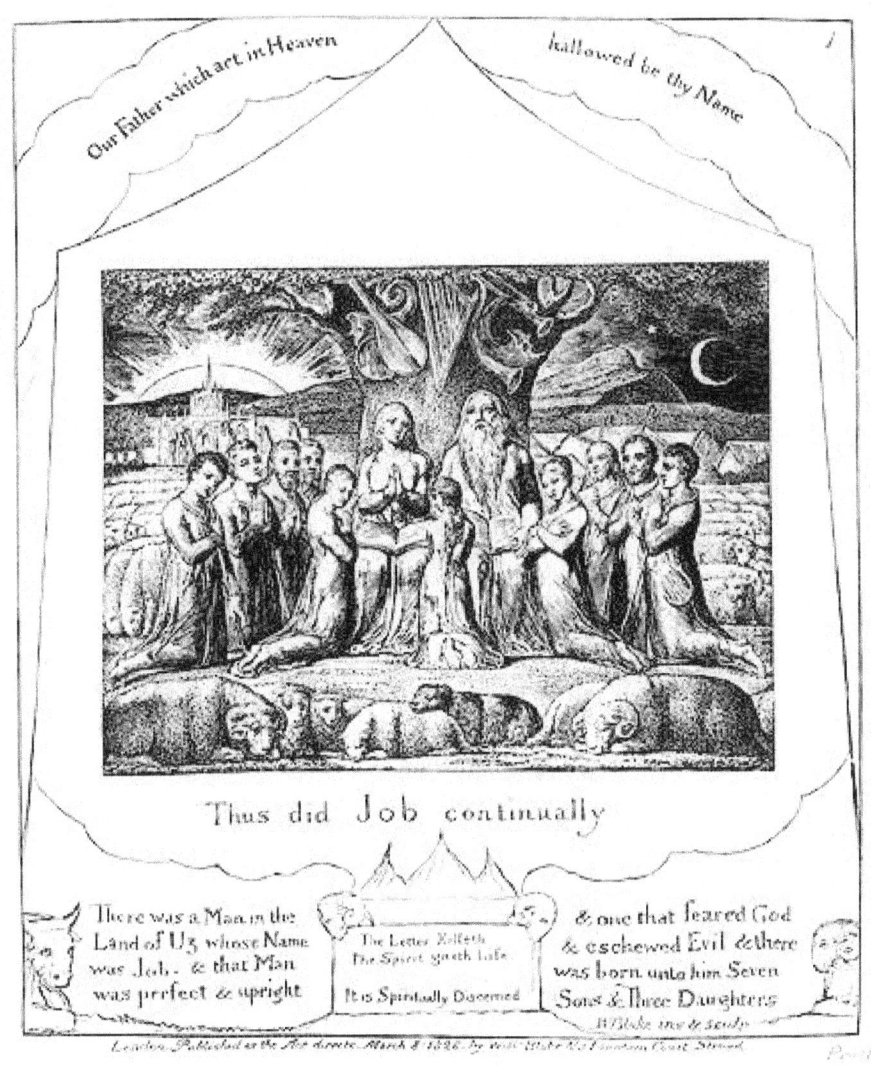

Our Father which art in Heaven   hallowed be thy Name

Thus did Job continually

There was a Man in the Land of Uz whose Name was Job, & that Man was perfect & upright

The Letter Killeth
The Spirit giveth Life

It is Spiritually Discerned

& one that feared God & eschewed Evil &there was born unto him Seven Sons &Three Daughters

W Blake inv & sculp

London Published as the Act directs March 8 1825 by Will Blake N 3 Fountain Court Strand

Our Father which art in Heaven hallowed be thy Name

Thus did Job continually

There was a Man in the

Land of Uz whose Name

was Job & that Man

was perfect & upright

The Letter Killeth

The Spirit giveth Life

It is Spiritually Discerned

& one that feared God

& one that eschewed Evil & there

was born unto him Seven

Sons & Three Daughters

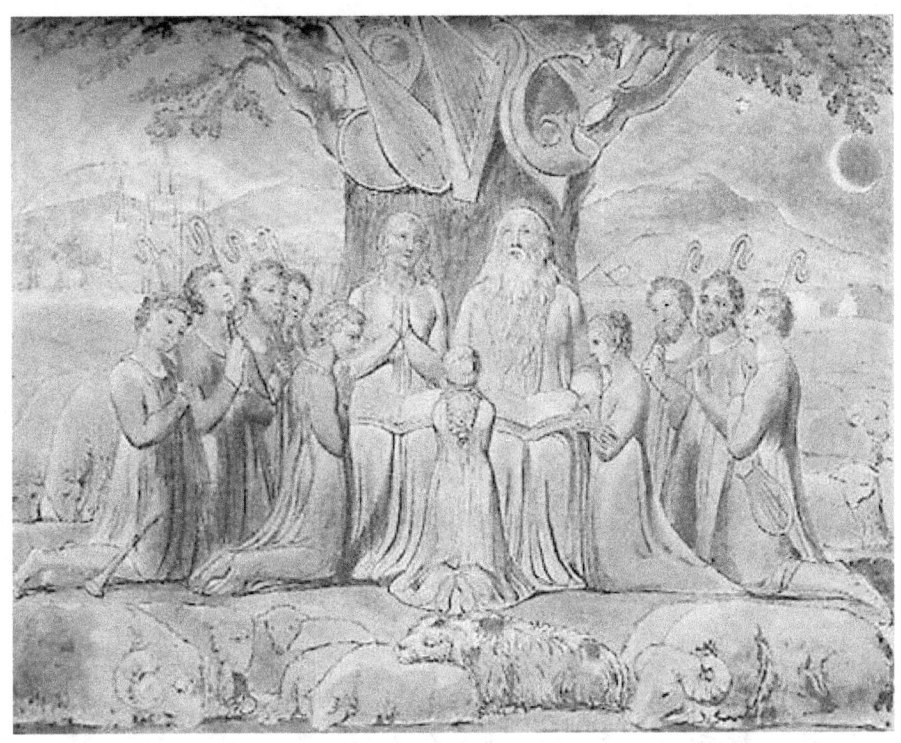

Job and his family

Our Father which art in heaven, Hallowed be thy name (Matthew 6: 9; Luke 11: 2:

Thus did Job continually (Job i:5)

There was a man in the land of Uz, whose name was Job; and that man was perfect and upright, and one that feared God, and eschewed evil. And there were born unto him seven sons and three daughters (Job 1: 1-2)

. . . the letter killeth, but the spirit giveth life (II Corinthians 3: 6:

. . . they are spiritually discerned (I Corinthians 2: 14:

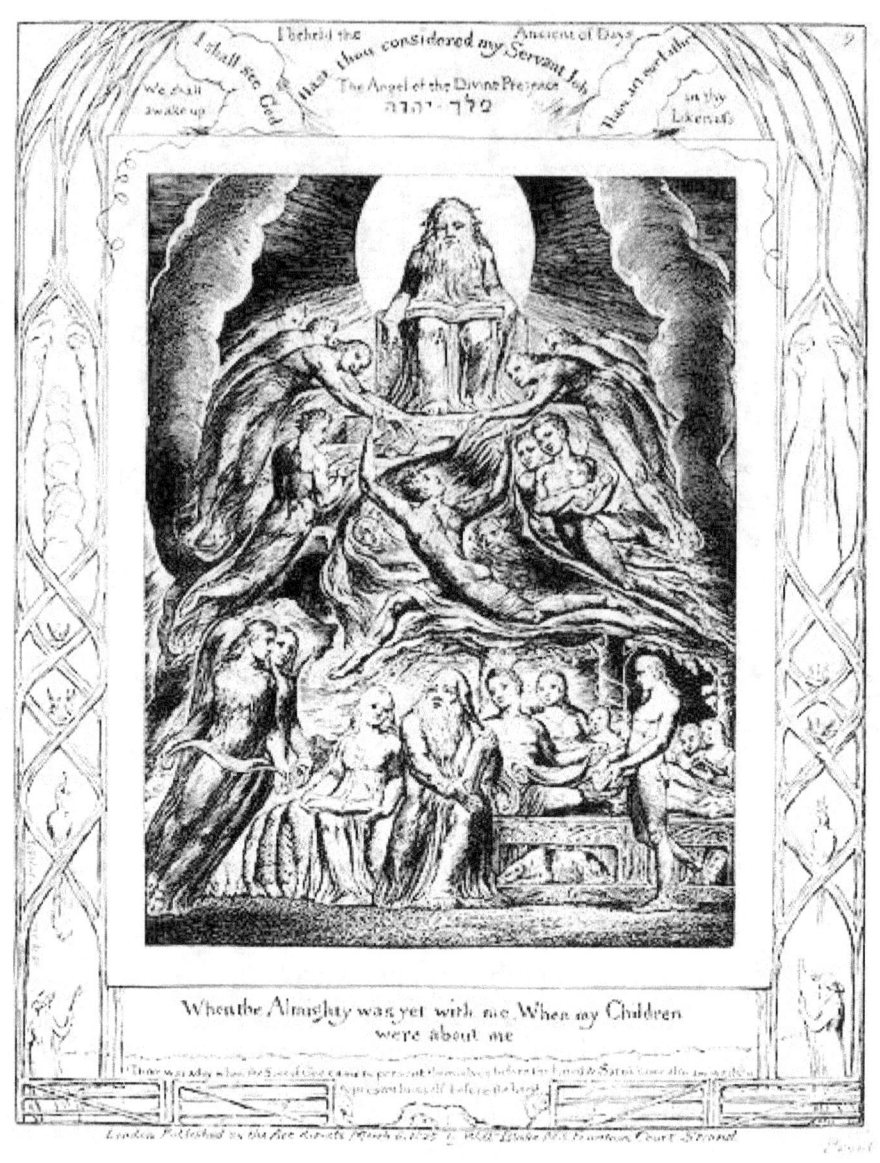

I beheld the

Ancient of Days

Hast thou considered my servant Job

The Angel of the Divine Presence

I shall see God

Thou art our Father

We shall awake up with thy Likeness

When the Almighty was yet with me, When my Children were about me

There was a day when the Sons of God came to present themselves before the Lord & Satan came also among them to present himself before the Lord.

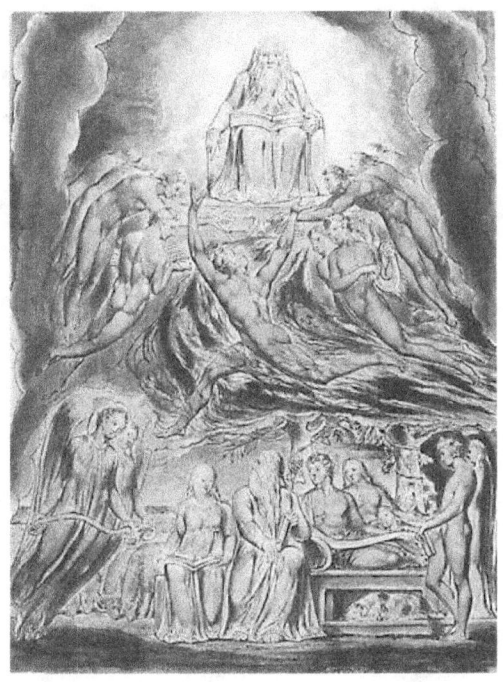

Satan before the throne of God

I beheld . . . the Ancient of days (Daniel 7:9)

Hast thou considered my servant Job (Job 1: 8)

Note: This phrase does not appear in the Bible. It signifies Satan, who presents himself before the Lord (Job 1: 6). The Hebrew letters beneath his name, however, identify him as "King Jehovah," Job's false God.

. . . shall I see God (Job 19: 26)

. . . thou art our father (Isaiah 64: 8)

. . . when I awake, with thy likeness (Psalm 17:19)

When the Almighty was yet with me, when my children were about me
(Job 29:5)

Now there was a day when the sons of God came to present themselves
before the Lord, and Satan came also among them (Job 1:6)

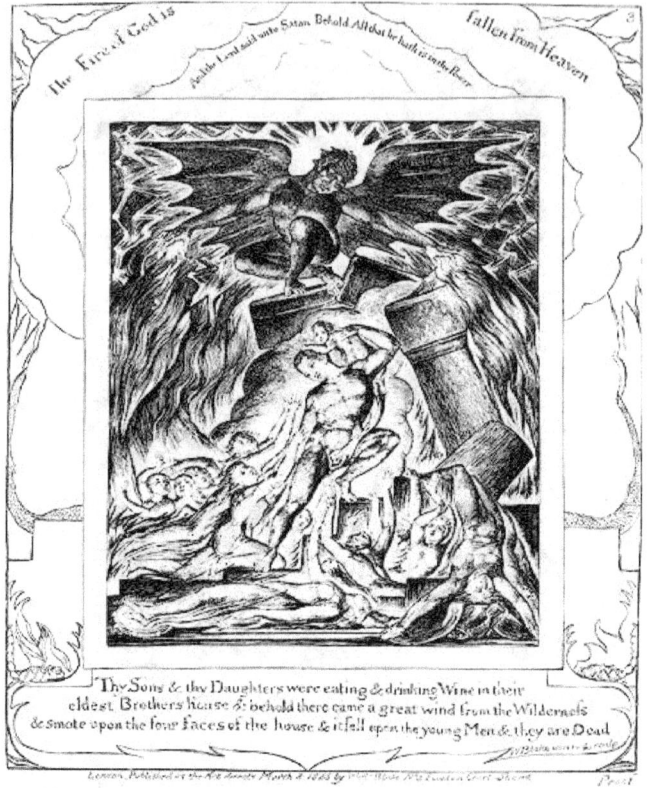

The Fire of God is

fallen from Heaven.

And the Lord said unto Satan Behold All that he hath is in thy Power

Thy Sons & thy Daughters were eating & drinking Wine in their eldest
Brothers house & behold there came a great wind from the Wilderness &

8

smote upon the four faces of the house & it fell upon the young Men & they are Dead

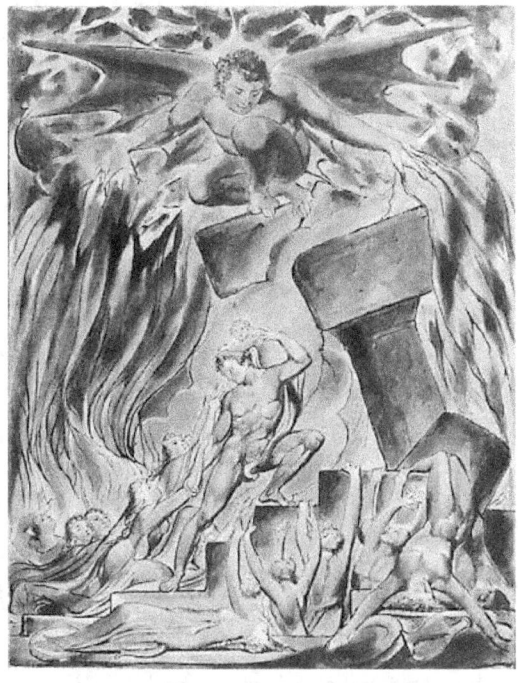

Job's sons and daughters destroyed

The fire of God is

fallen from Heaven (Job 1:12)

And the Lord said unto Satan, Behold, all that he hath is in thy power (Job 1:12)

Thy sons and thy daughters were eating and drinking wine in their eldest brother's house: And, behold, there came a great wind from the wilderness, and smote the four corners of the house, and it fell upon the young men, and they are dead (Job 1:18-19)

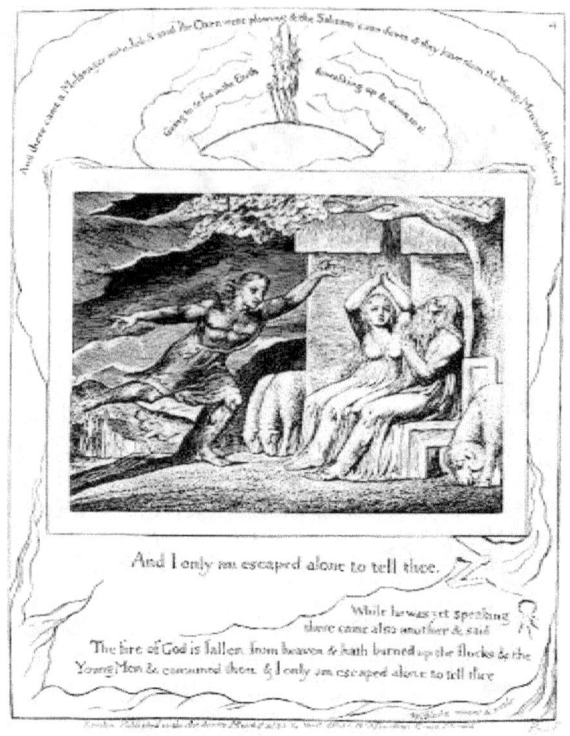

And there came a Messenger unto Job & said The Oxen were plowing & the Sabeans came down & they have slain the Young Men with the Sword

Going to & fro in the Earth

& walking up & down in it

And I only am escaped alone to tell thee

While he was yet speaking there came also another & said

The fire of God is fallen from heaven & hath burned up the flocks & the

Young Men & consumed then; and I only am escaped alone to tell thee

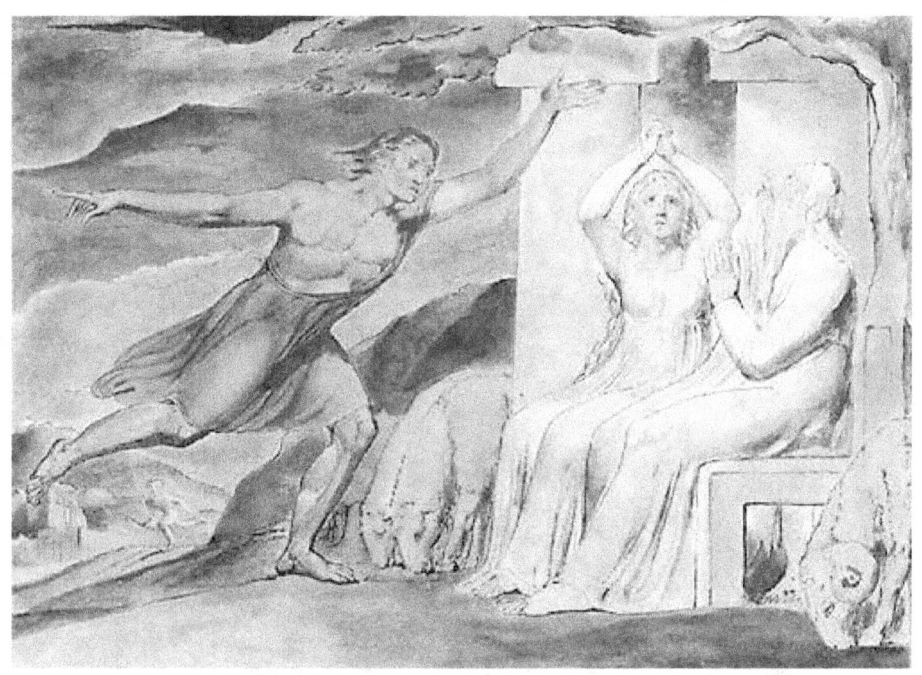

The messengers tell Job of his misfortunes

And there came a Messenger unto Job, and said, The Oxen were plowing
. . . And the Sabeans fell upon them . . . yea, they have slain the servants
with the edge of the sword (Job 1:14-15)

From going to and fro in the earth, and from walking up and down in it
(Job 1:7)

. . . and I only am escaped alone to tell thee (Job 1:15)

While he was yet speaking, there came also another, and said, The fire of
God is fallen from heaven, and hath burned up the sheep, and the servants,
and consumed them, and I only am escaped alone to tell thee (Job 1:16)

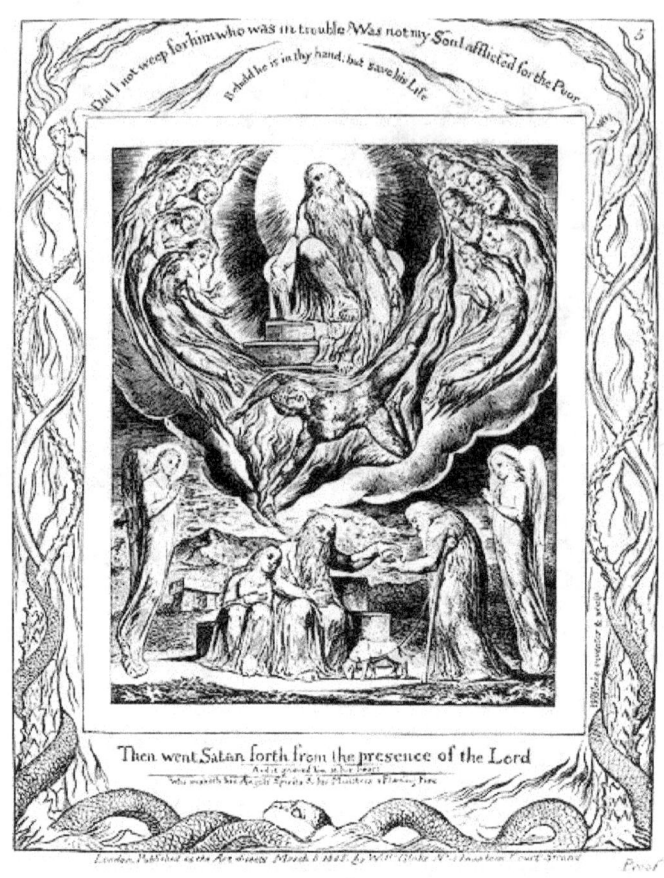

Did I not weep for him who was in trouble? Was not my Soul afflicted for the Poor

Behold he is in thy hand: but save his Life

Then went Satan forth from the presence of the Lord

And it grieved him at his heart

Who maketh his Angels Spirits & his Ministers a Flaming Fire

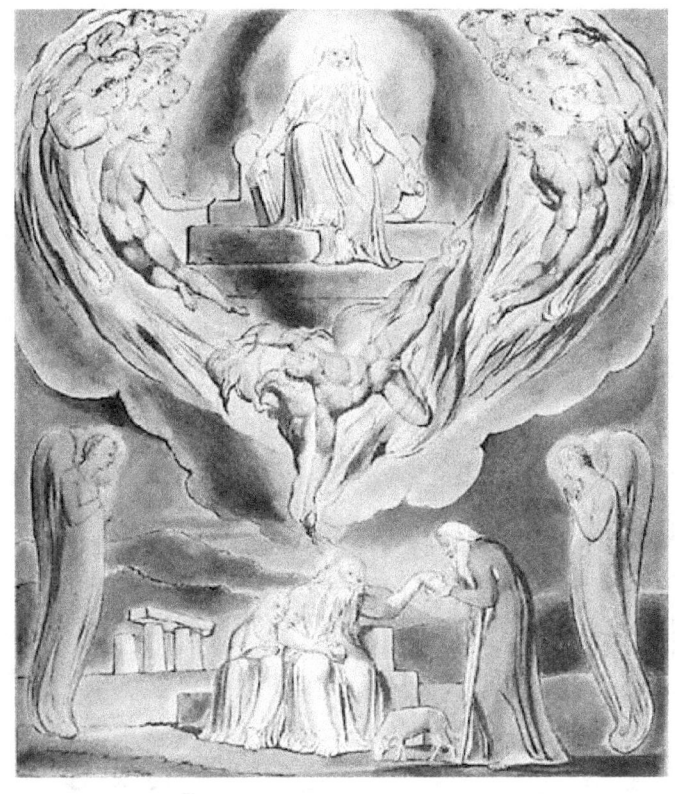

Satan going forth from the presence of the Lord

Did not I weep for him that was in trouble? was not my soul grieved for the poor? (Job 30:25)

Behold he is in thine hand; but save his life (Job 2:6)

So Satan went forth from the presence of the Lord (Job 1:12)

. . . and it grieved him at his heart (Genesis 6:6)

Who maketh his angels spirits; his ministers a flaming fire (Psalm 104:4)

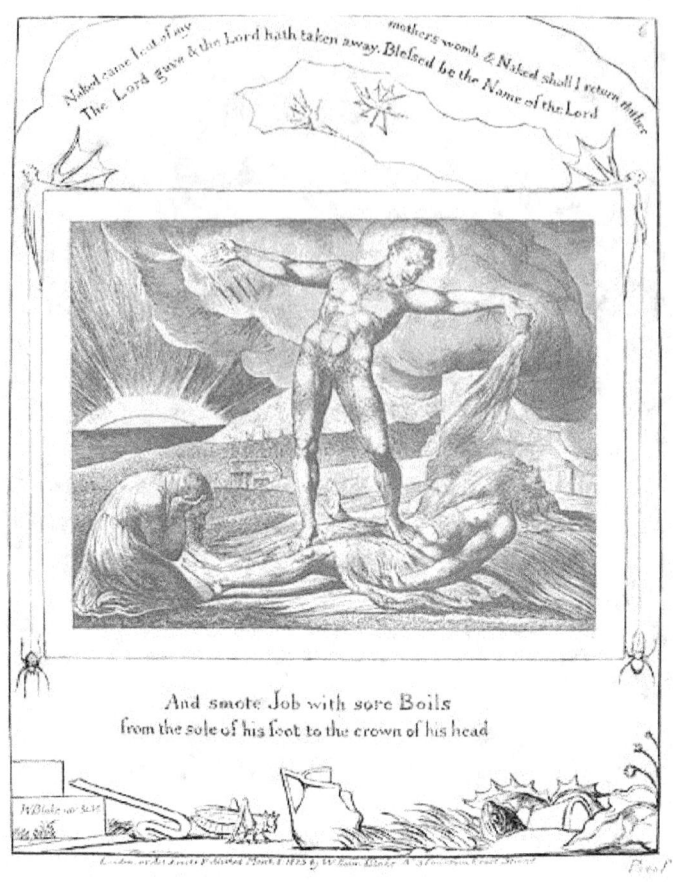

Naked came I out of my

mothers womb & Naked shall I return thither

The Lord gave & the Lord hath taken away, Blessed be the Name of the Lord.

. . . and smote Job with sore Boils

from the sole of his foot to the crown of his head

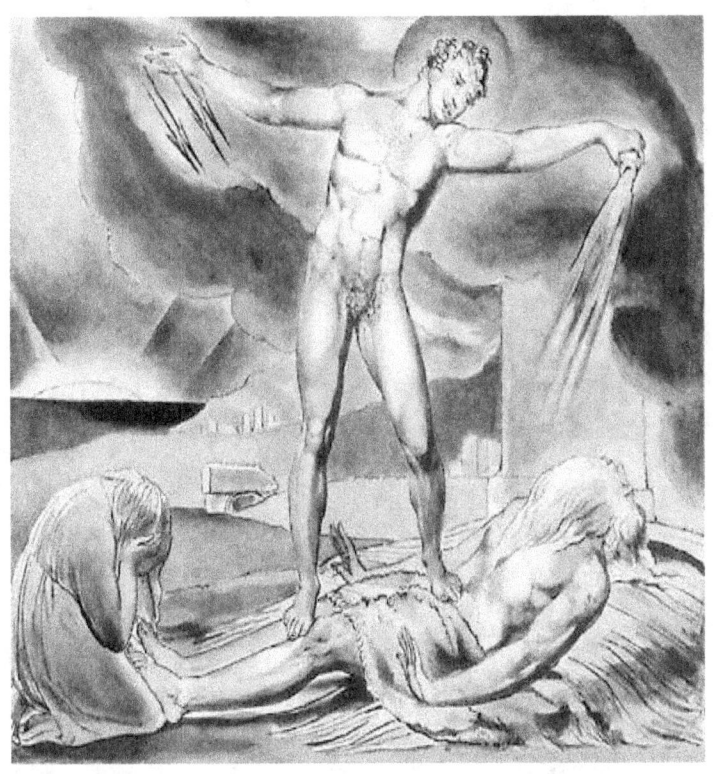

Satan smiting Job with boils

Naked came I out of my

mother's womb, and naked shall I return thither: The Lord gave, and the
Lord hath taken away, Blessed be the Name of the Lord (Job 1:21)

. . . and smote Job with sore boils from the sole of his foot unto his crown
(Job 2:7)

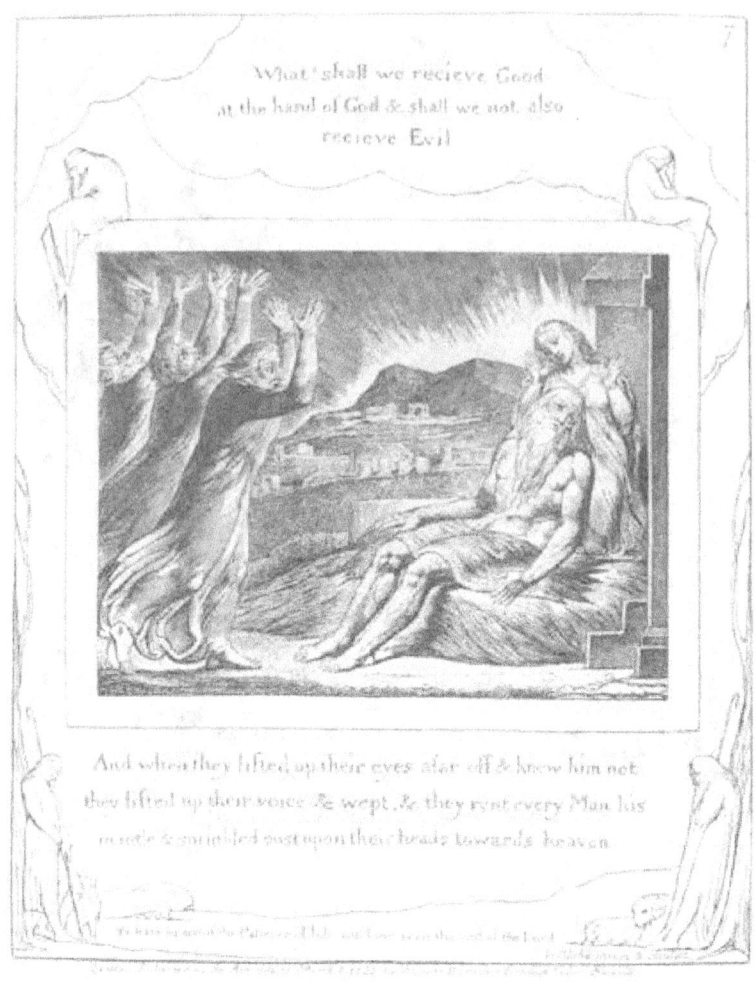

What! shall we recieve Good at the hand of God & shall we not also
recieve Evil

And when they lifted up their eyes afar off & knew him not

they lifted up their voice & wept, & they rent every Man his

mantle & sprinkled dust upon their heads towards heaven

Ye have heard of the Patience of Job and have seen the end of the Lord.

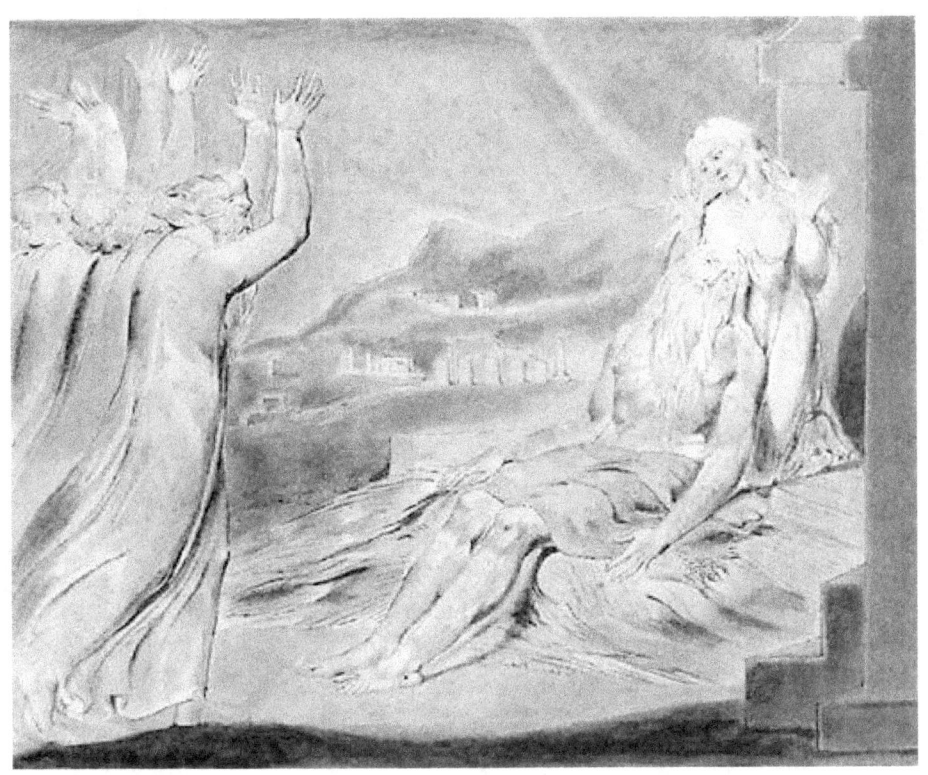

Job's comforters

What? shall we receive good at the hand of God, and shall we not receive
evil? (Job 2:10)

And when they lifted up their eyes afar off, and knew him not, they lifted
up their voice, and wept; and they rent every one his mantle, and
sprinkled dust upon their heads towards heaven (Job 2:12)

Ye have heard of the Patience of Job and have seen the end of the Lord.

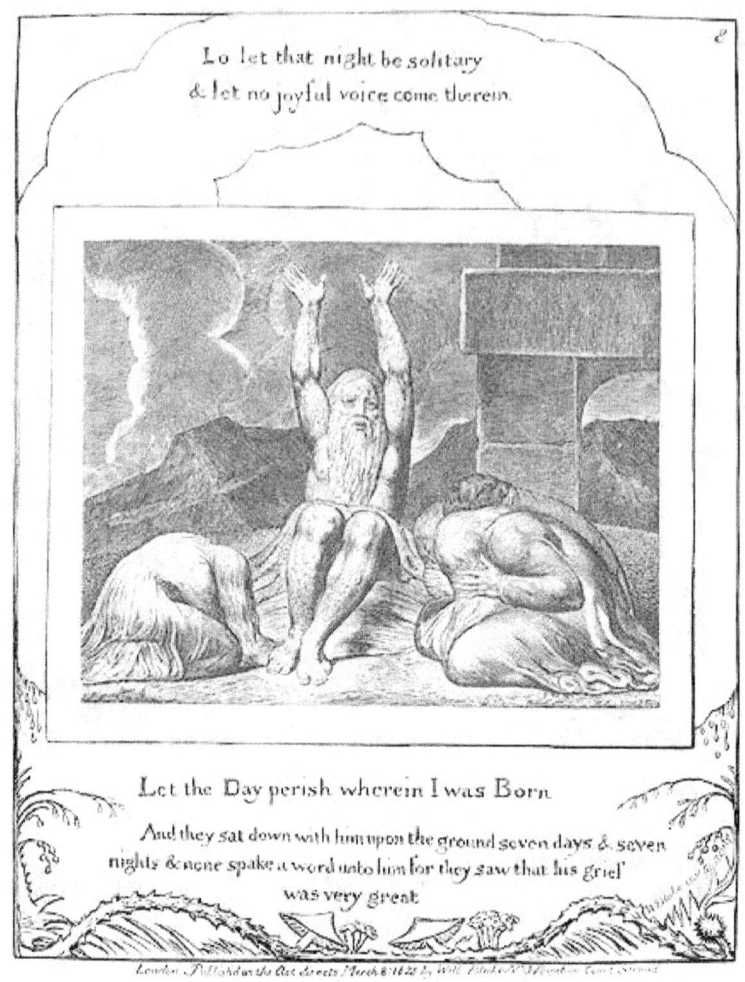

Lo let that night be solitary

and let no joyful voice come therein

Let the Day perish wherein I was Born

And they sat down with him upon the ground seven days & seven

nights & none spake a word unto him for they saw that his grief

was very great

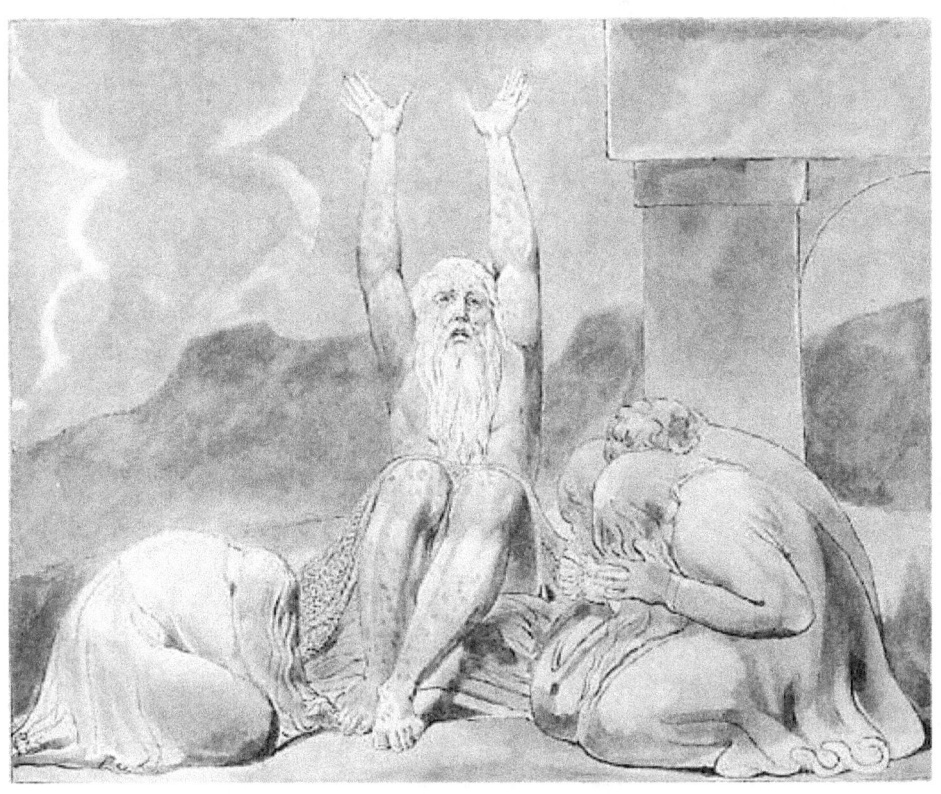

Job's despair

Lo, let that night be solitary, let no joyful voice come therein (Job 3:7)

Let the day perish wherein I was born (Job 3:3)

So they sat down with him upon the ground seven days and seven nights,
and none spake a word unto him: for they saw that his grief was very great
(Job 2:13)

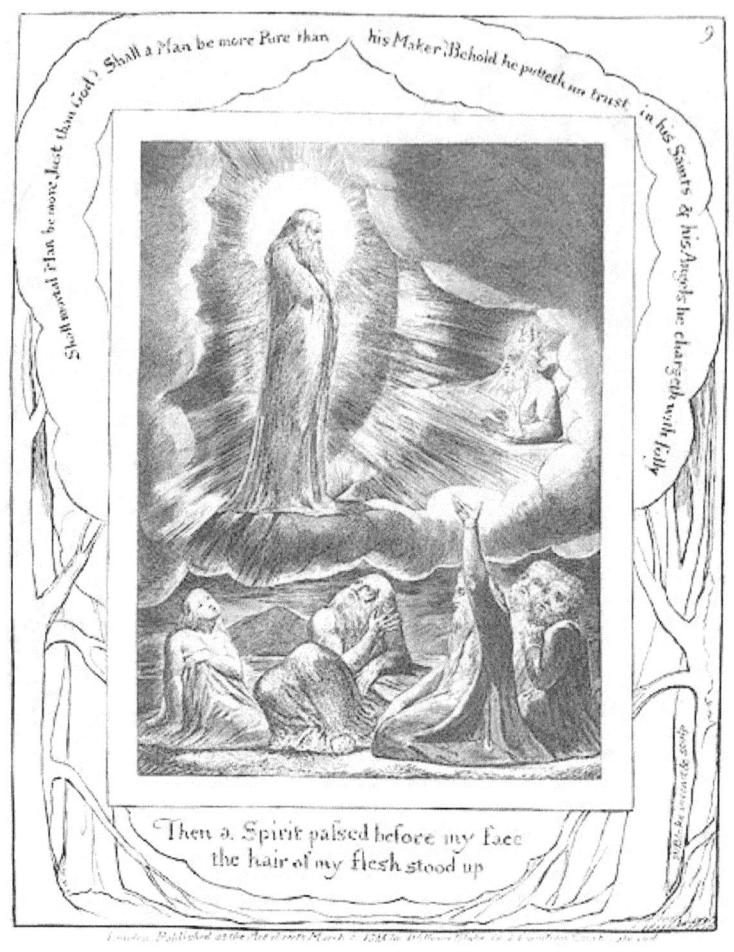

Shall mortal Man be more Just than God? Shall a Man be more Pure than his Maker? Behold he putteth no trust in his Saints & his Angels he chargeth with folly

Then a Spirit passed before my face

the hair of my flesh stood up

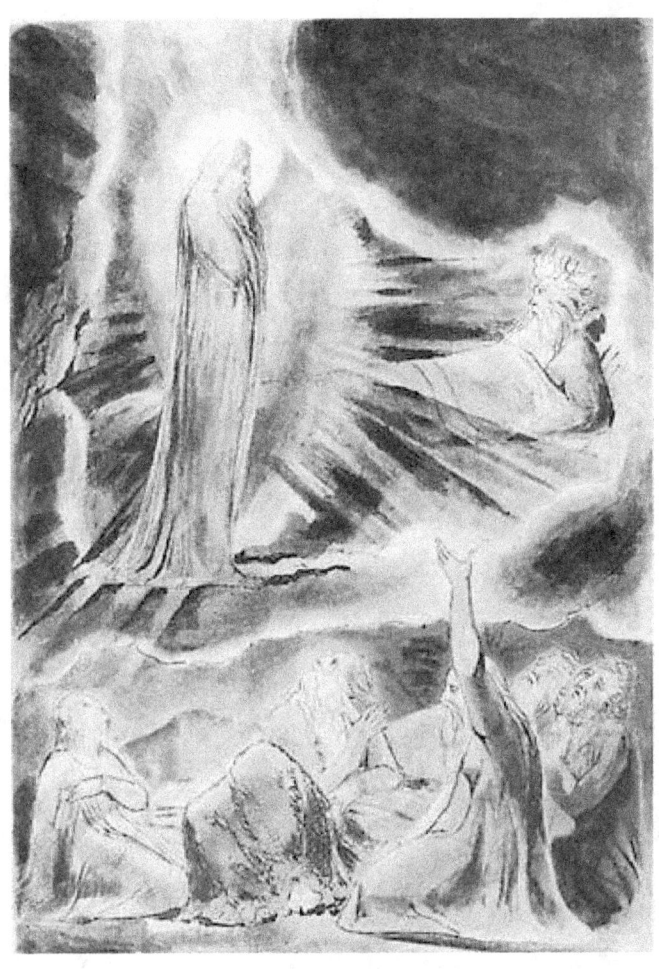

The vision of Eliphaz

Shall mortal man be more just than God? shall a man be more pure than his maker? Behold he putt no trust in his servants; and his angels he charged with folly (Job 4:17-18)

Then a Spirit passed before my face; the hair of my flesh stood up (Job 4:15)

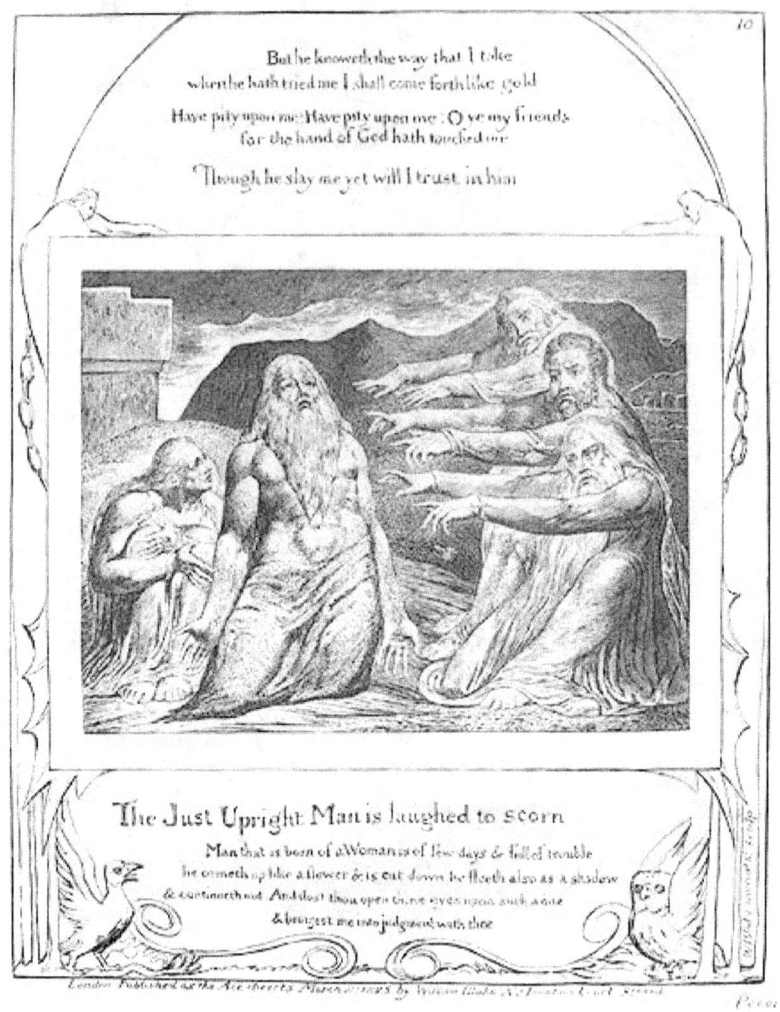

But he knoweth the way that I take

when he hath tried me I shall come forth like gold

Have pity upon me! Have pity upon me! O ye my friends for the hand of God hath touched me

Though he slay yet will I trust in him

The Just Upright Man is laughed to scorn

Man that is born of a Woman is of few days & full of trouble he cometh up like a flower & is cut down, he fleeth also as a shadow

& continueth not. And dost thou open thine eyes upon such a one

& bringest me into judgment with thee

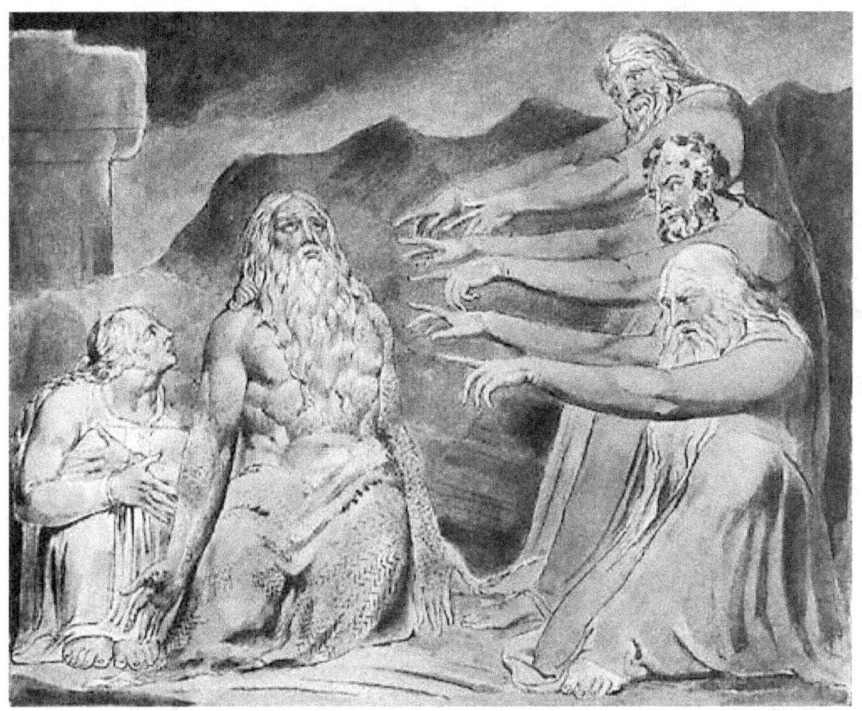

Job rebuked by his friends

But he knoweth the way that I take: when he hath tried me, I shall come
forth as gold (Job 23:10)

Have pity upon me! Have pity upon me! O ye my friends for the hand of
God hath touched me (Job 19:21)

Though he slay me, yet will I trust in him (Job 12:4)

. . . the just upright man is laughed to scorn (Job 12:4)

Man that is born of a woman is of few days, and full of trouble. He cometh
forth like a flower, and is cut down: he fleeth also as a shadow, and

continueth not. And dost thou open thine eyes upon such an one, and bringest me into judgment with thee? (Job 14:1-3)

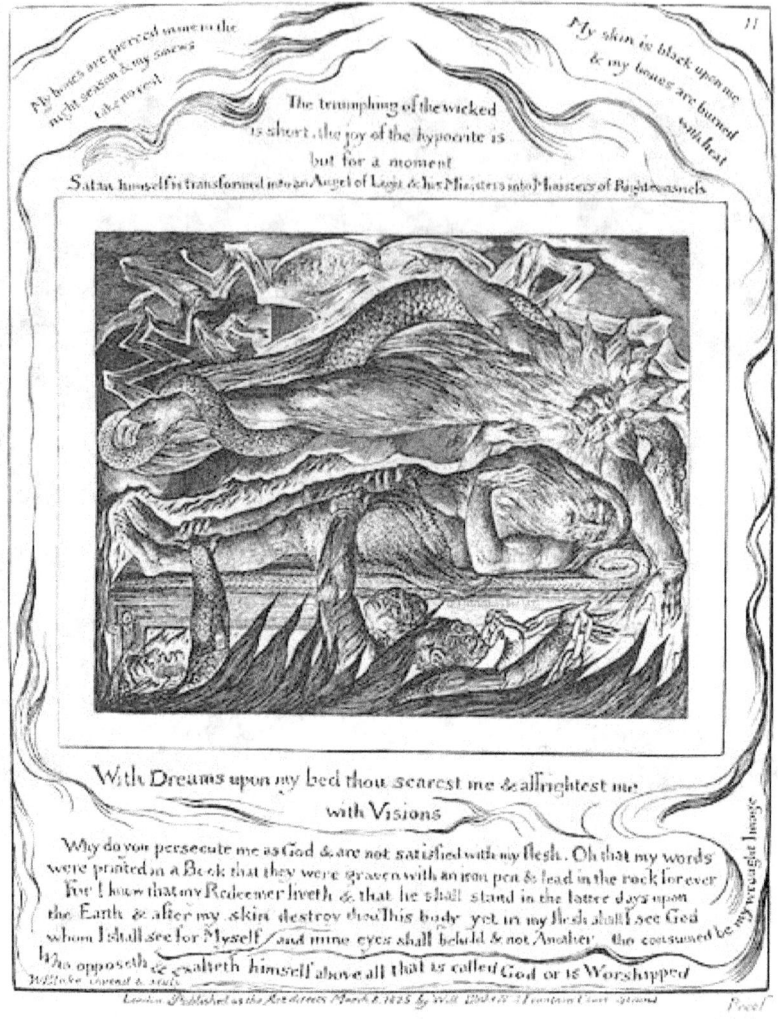

My bones are pierced me in the

night season & my sinews

take no rest

My skin is black upon me, and

& my bones are burned

with heat

The triumphing of the wicked

is short, the joy of the hypocrite is

but for a moment

Satan himself is transformed into an Angel of Light & his Ministers into Ministers of Righteousness

With Dreams upon my bed thou scarest me & affrightest me with Visions

Why do you persecute me as God & are not satisfied with my flesh. Oh that my words were printed in a Book that they were graven with an iron pen & lead in the rock for ever For I know that my Redeemer liveth & that he shall stand in the latter days upon the Earth & after my skin destroy thou This body yet in my flesh shall I see God whom I shall see for Myself and mine Eyes shall behold & not Another tho consumed be my wrought Image

Who opposeth & exalteth himself above all that is called God or is Worshipped

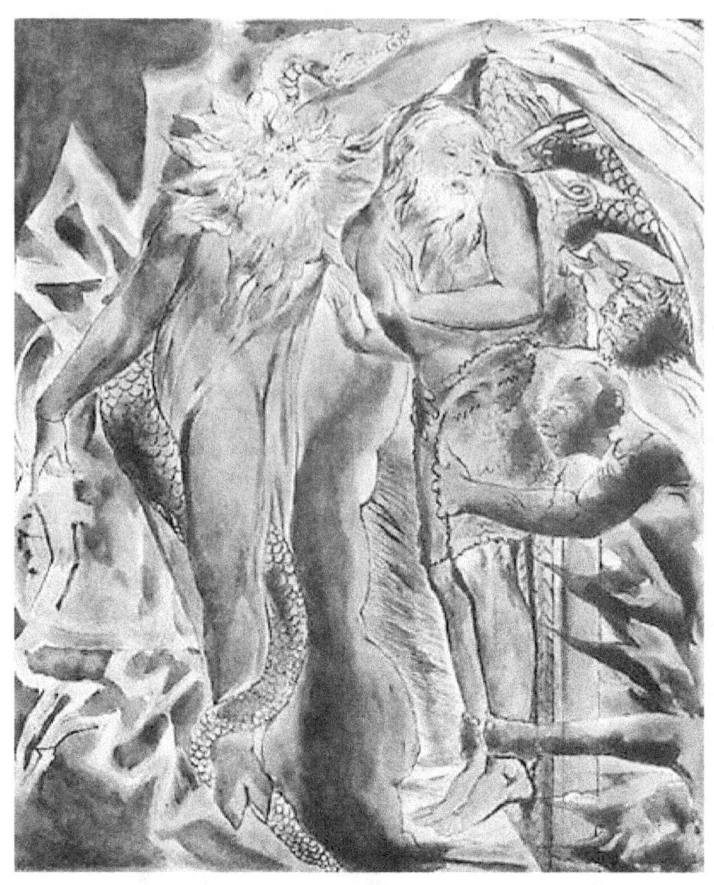

Job's dreams

My bones are pierced in me in the night season: and my sinews take no rest (Job 30:17)

My skin is black upon me, and my bones are burned with heat (Job 30:30)

. . . the triumphing of the wicked is short, and the joy of the hypocrite but for a moment (Job 20:5)

. . . for Satan himself is transformed into an angel of light . . . his ministers also be transformed as the ministers of righteousness (II Corinthians 11:14-15)

Then thou scarest me with dreams, and terrifiest me through visions (Job 7:14)

Why do ye persecute me as God, and are not satisfied with my flesh? Oh that my words were now written! oh that they were printed in a book! That they were graven with an iron pen and lead in the rock for ever! For I know that my redeemer liveth, and that he shall stand at the latter day upon the earth: And though after my skin worms destroy this body, yet in my flesh shall I see God: Whom I shall see for myself, and mine eyes shall behold, and not another; though my reins be consumed within me (Job 19:22-27)

Who opposeth & exalteth himself above all that is called God, or is worshipped (II Thessalonians 2:4)

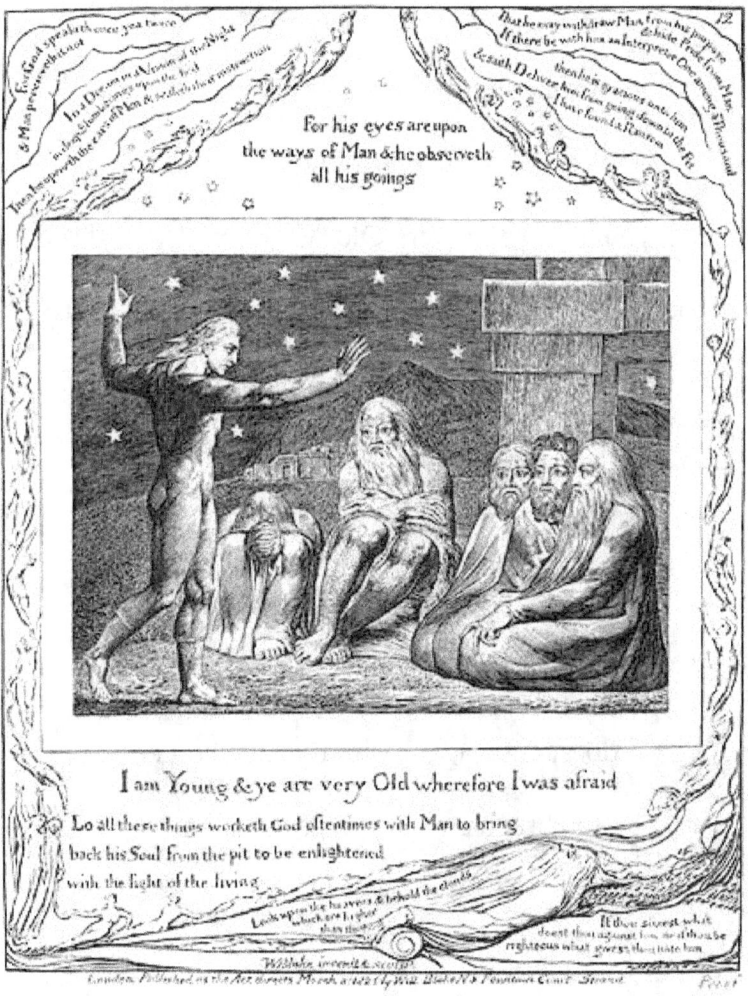

For God speaketh once yea twice

& Man percieveth it not

In a Dream in a Vision of the Night

in deep Slumberings upon the bed

Then he openeth the ears of Men & sealeth their instruction

That he may withdraw Man from his purpose

& hide Pride from Man

For his eyes are upon

the says of Man & he observeth

all his goings

I am young & ye are very Old wherefore I was afraid

Lo all these things worketh God oftentimes with Man to bring

back his Soul from the pit to be enlightened

with the light of the living

Look unto the heavens & behold the clouds

which are higher than thou

If thou sinnest, what

doest thou against him? . . . If thou be

righteous, what givest thou him?

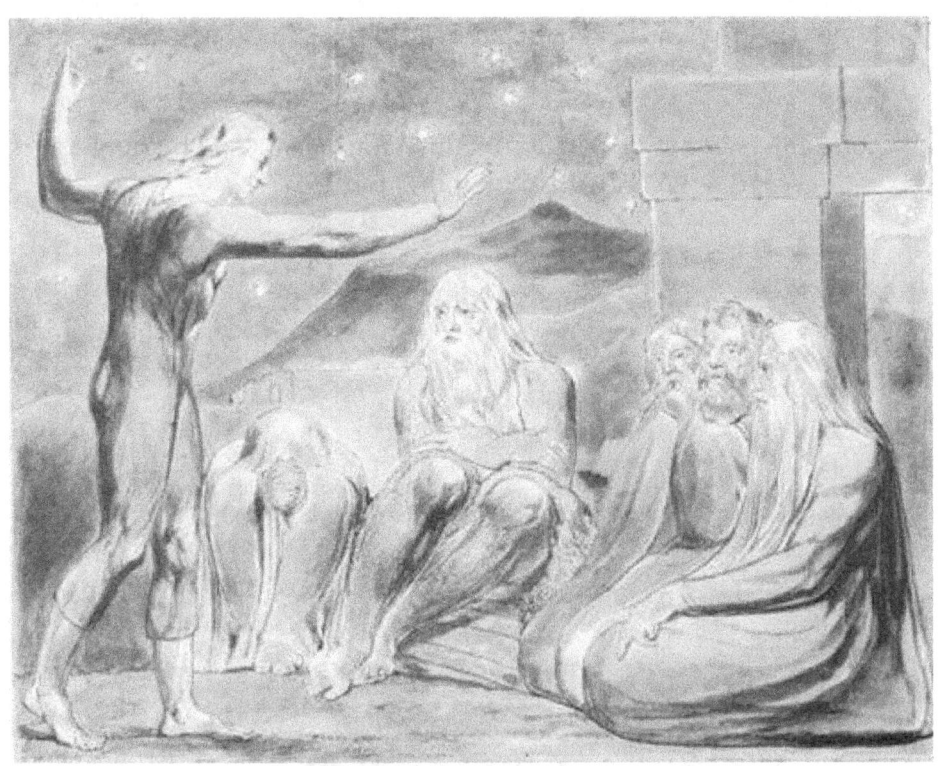

The wrath of Elihu

For God speaketh once, yea twice, yet man perceiveth it not (Job 33:14)

In a dream, in a vision of the night, when deep sleep falleth upon men, in slumberings upon the bed (Job 33:15)

Then he openeth the ears of men, and sealeth their instruction (Job 33:16)

That he may withdraw man from his purpose, and hide pride from man. (Job 33:17)

For his eyes are upon the ways of man, and he seeth all his goings (Job 34:21)

I am young, and ye are very old; wherefore I was afraid (Job 32:6)

Lo, all these things worketh God oftentimes with man, To bring back his soul from the pit, to be enlightened with the light of the living (Job 33: 29-30)

Look unto the heavens, and see; and behold the clouds which are higher than thou (Job 34: 5)

If thou sinnest, what doest thou against him? . . . If thou be righteous, what givest thou him? (Job 35:6-7)

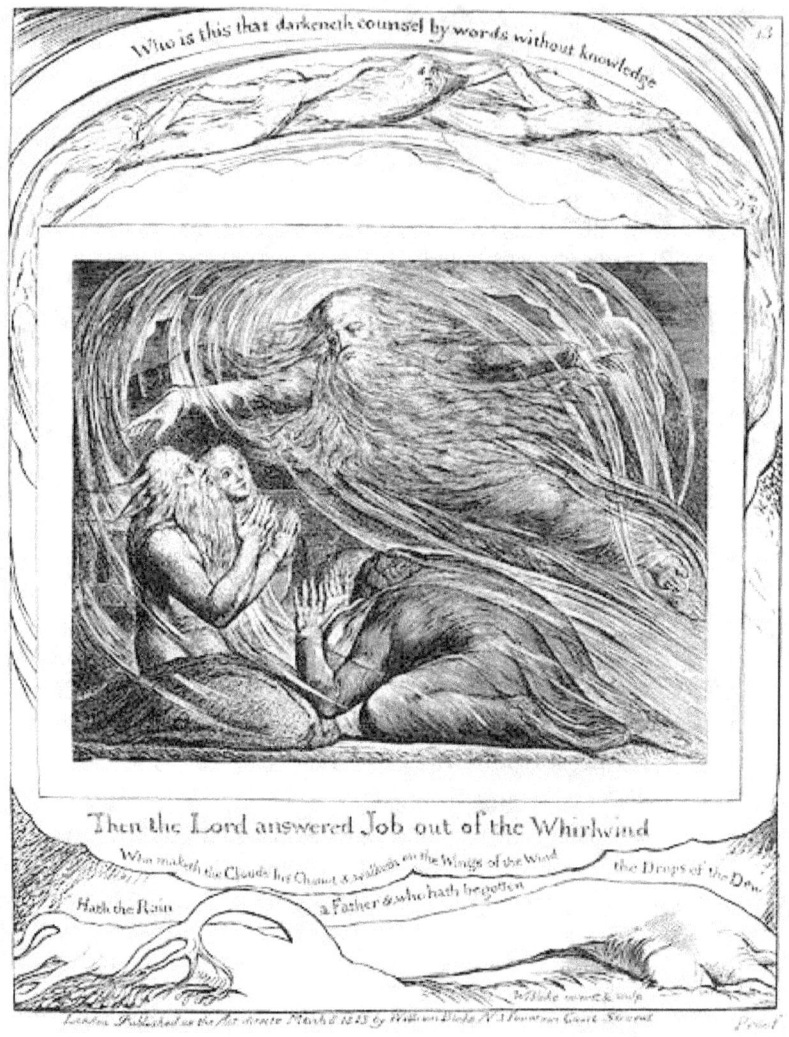

Who is this that darkeneth counsel by words without knowledge

Then the Lord answered Job out of the Whirlwind

Who maketh the Clouds his Chariot & walketh on the Wings of the Wind

Hath the Rain a Father & who hath begotten the Drops of the Dew

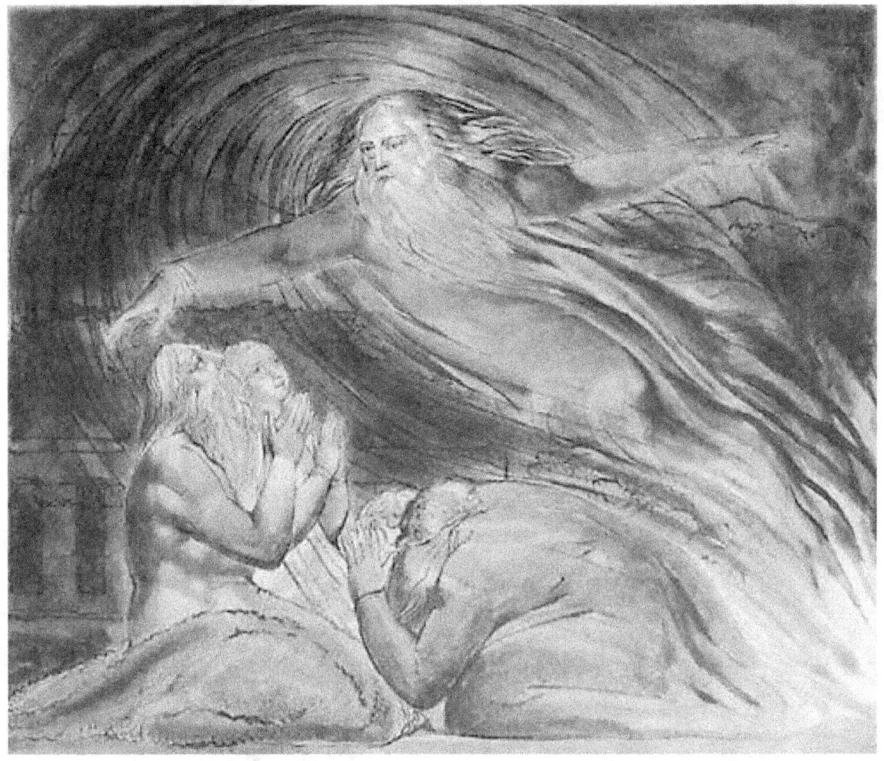

The Lord answering Job out of the whirlwind

Who is this that darkeneth counsel by words without knowledge? (Job 38:2)

Then the Lord answered Job out of the whirlwind (Job 38:1)

. . . who maketh the clouds his chariot: who walketh on the wings of the wind (Psalm 104:3)

Hath the rain a Father? or who hath begotten the drops of the dew? (Job 38:28)

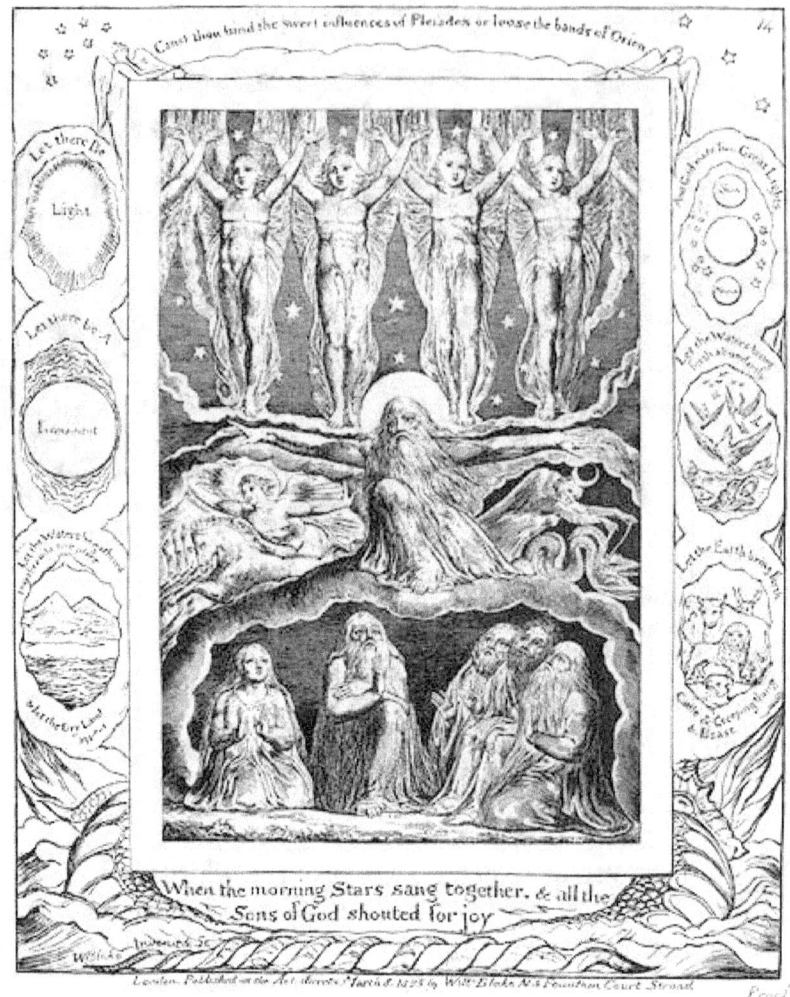

Canst thou bind the sweet influences of Pleiades or loose the bands of
Orion

When the morning stars sang together & all the

sons of God shouted for joy

Let there Be

Light

Let there be A

Firmament

Let the waters be gathered

together into one place, and

& let the Dry Land

appear

And God made Two Great Lights

Sun

Moon

Let the Waters bring

forth abundantly

Let the earth bring forth

Cattle & Creeping thing

& Beast

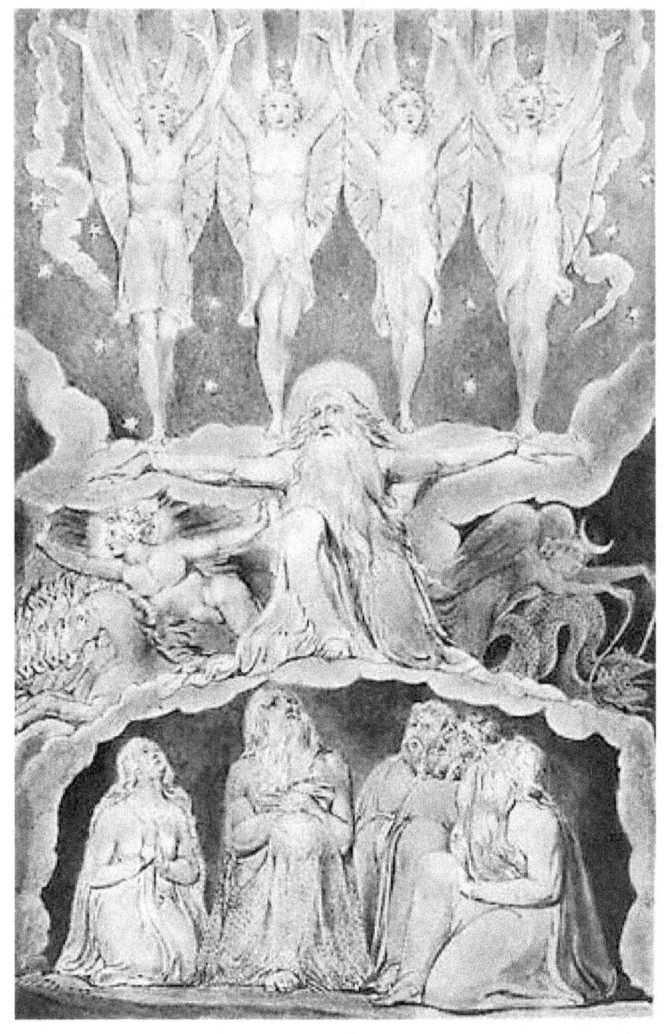

When the morning stars sang together

Canst thou bind the sweet influences of Pleiades, or loose the bands of Orion? (Job 38:31)

When the morning stars sang together, and all the sons of God shouted for joy (Job 38:7)

Let there be light (Genesis 1:3)

Let there be a firmament (Genesis 1:6)

Let the waters under the heaven be gathered together unto one place, and
let the dry land appear (Genesis 1:9)

And God made two great lights (Genesis 1:16)

Let the waters bring forth abundantly (Genesis 1:20)

Let the earth bring forth the living creatures . . . cattle, and creeping thing,
the beasts of the earth (Genesis 1:24)

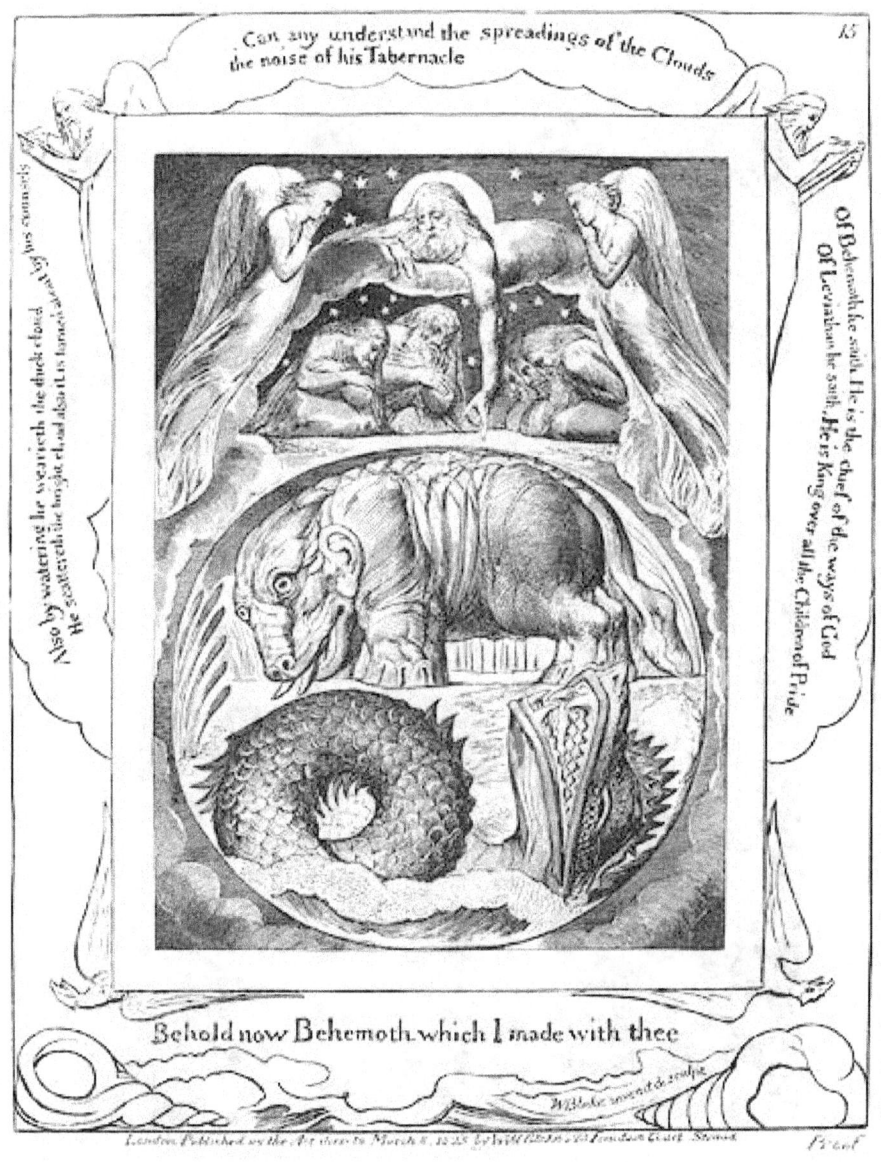

Can any understand the spreadings of the Clouds the noise of his
Tabernacle

Also by watering he wearieth the thick cloud

He scattereth the bright cloud also it is turned about by his counsels

Of Behemoth he saith, He is the chief of the ways of God

Of Leviathan he saith, He is King over all the Children of Pride

Behold now Behemoth which I made with thee

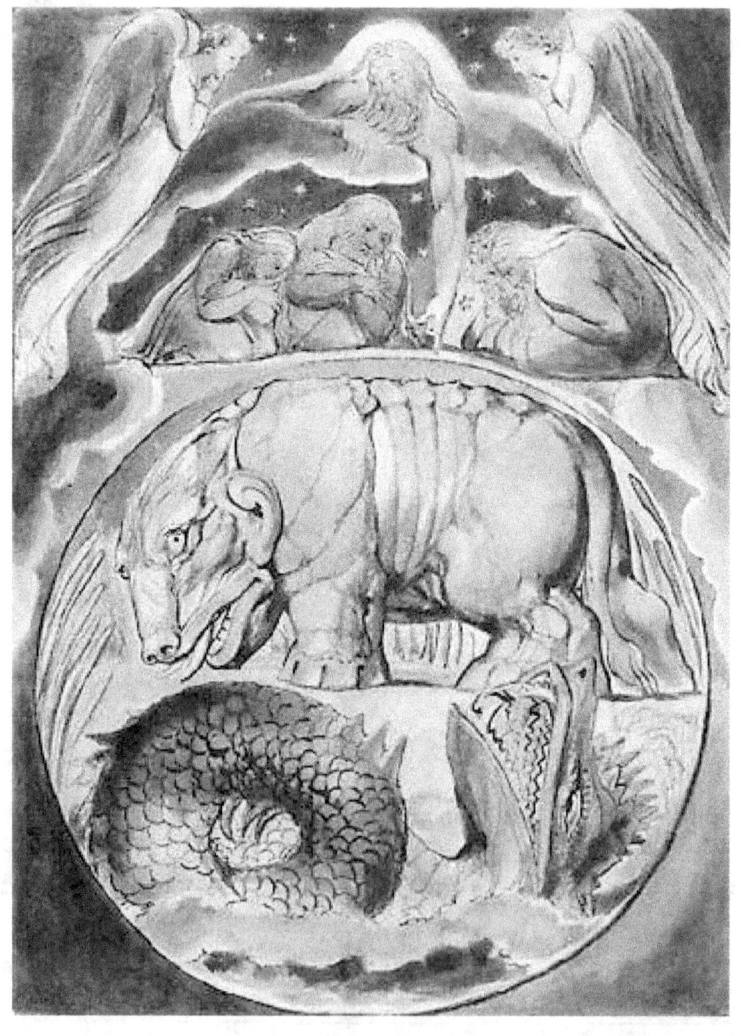

Behemoth and Leviathan

Also can any understand the spreadings of the clouds, or the noise of his tabernacle? (Job 36:29)

Also by watering he wearieth the thick cloud: he scattereth his bright cloud: And it is turned round about by his counsels (Job 37:11-12)

Behold now behemoth . . . He is the chief of the ways of God (Job 40:15, 19)

. . . he is a king over all the children of pride (Job 41: 34)

Behold now behemoth, which I made with thee (Job 40:15)

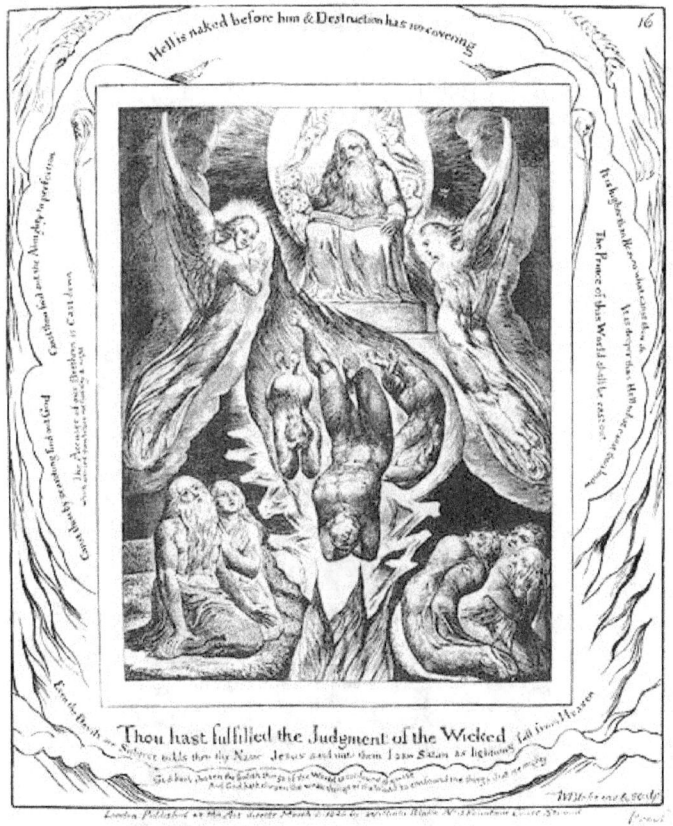

Hell is naked before him & destruction has no covering

Canst thou by searching find out God

Canst thou find out the Almighty to perfection

The Accuser of our Brethren is Cast down

which accused them before our God day & night

It is higher than Heaven what canst thou do

It is deeper than Hell what canst thou know

The prince of this World shall be cast out

Thou hast fulfilled the Judgment of the Wicked

Even the devils are Subject to Us thro thy Name. Jesus said unto them, I
saw Satan as lightning fall from Heaven

God hath chosen the foolish things of the World to confound the wise

And God hath chosen the weak things of the world to confound the
things which are mighty

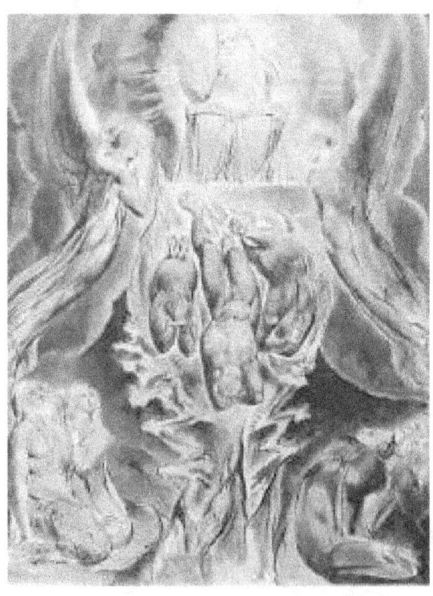

The fall of Satan

Hell is naked before him, and destruction hath no covering (Job 26:6)

Canst thou by searching find out God? canst thou find out the Almighty unto perfection? (Job 11:7)

... the accuser of our brethren is cast down, which accused them before our God day and night (Revelation 12:10)

It is as high as heaven; what canst thou do? deeper than hell, what canst thou know? (Job 11:8).

..now shall the prince of this world be cast out (John 12:31)

But thou hast fulfilled the judgment of the wicked (Job 36:17)

... even the devils are subject unto us through thy name. And he said unto them, I beheld Satan as lightning fall from heaven (Luke 10:17-18)

But God hath chosen the foolish things of the world to confound the wise; and God hath chosen the weak things of the world to confound the things which are mighty (I Corinthians 1:17)

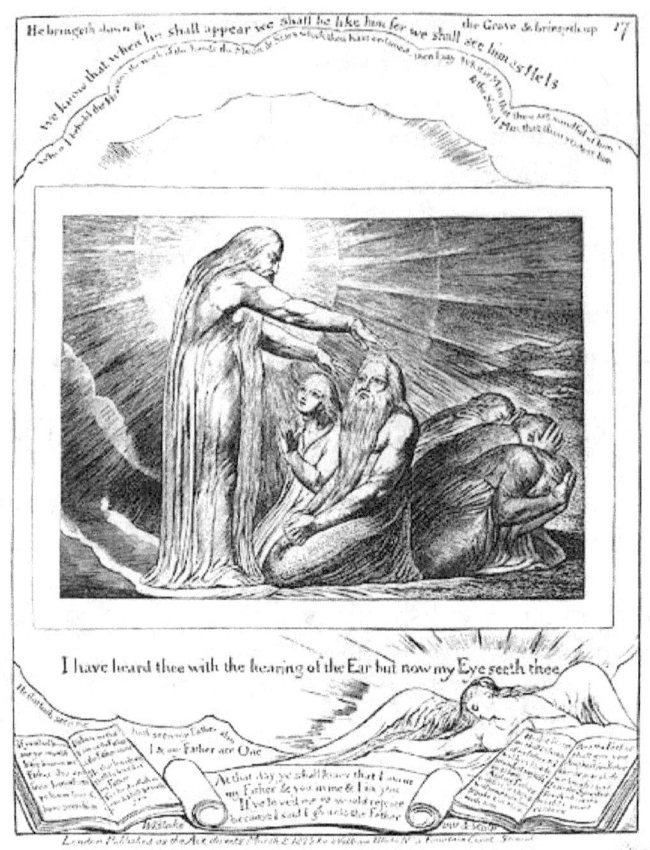

He bringeth down to

the Grave & bringeth up

we know that when he shall appear, we shall be like him for we shall see him as He Is.

When I behold the Heavens the work of thy hands the Moon & Stars which thou hast ordained, then I say, What is Man that thou art mindful of him?

& the Son of Man that thou visitest him

I have heard thee with the hearing of the Ear but now my Eye seeth thee

He that seen me

hath seen my Father also

I & my Father are One

If ye had know me,

ye should have known my

Father also and

from henceforth

ye know him &

have seen him

Believe me that

I am in the Father

& the Father in me

He that loveth me

shall be loved of

my Father

For he dwelleth in

you & shall be with

you

At that day ye shall know that I am in

my Father & you in me & I in you

If ye loved me ye would rejoice

because I said I go unto the Father

He that loveth

me shall be loved

of my Father & I

will love him &

manifest myself

unto him

And the Father

will love him & we

will come unto him, and

& make our abode with him

And the Father . . .

shall give you

Another Comforter, t

that he may abide

with you for ever

Even the Spirit of truth whom the World Cannot recieve

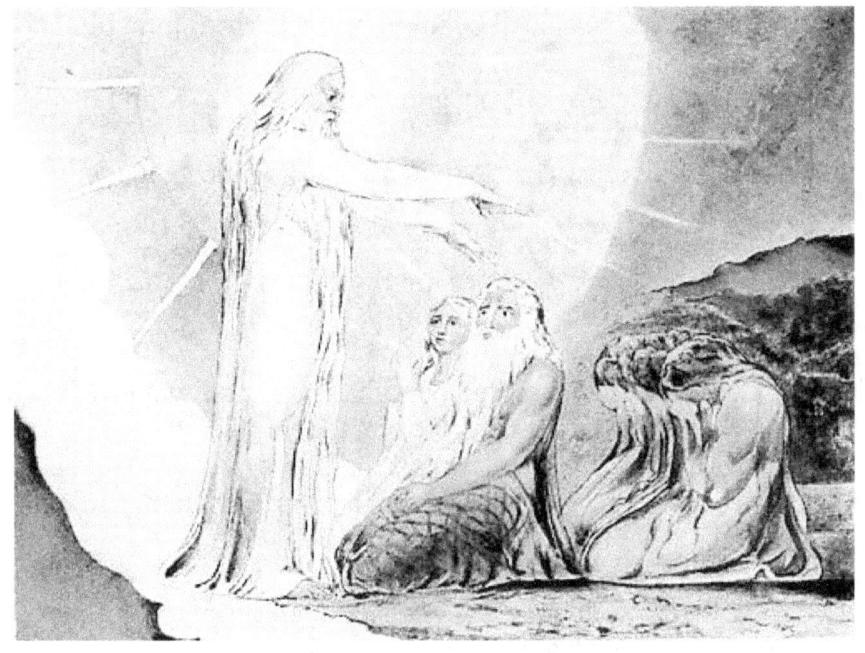

The vision of Christ

. . . he bringeth down to the grave, and bringeth up (I Samuel 2:6)

. . . we know that, when he shall appear, we shall be like him; for we shall see him as he is. (I John 3:2)

When I consider thy heaven, the work of the finger, the moon and the stars, which thou hast ordained, What is man, that thou art mindful of him? and the son of man, that thou visitest him? (Psalm 8:3-4)

I have heard of thee with the hearing of the ear; but now mine eye seeth thee (Job 42:5)

. . . he that hath seen me hath seen the Father (John 14:9)

I and my Father are one (John 10:30)

If ye had know me, ye should have known my Father also: and from henceforth ye know him, and have seen him (John 14:21)

Believe me that I am in the Father, and the Father in me (John 14:11)

. . . he that loveth me shall be loved of my Father (John 14:21)

. . . for he dwelleth with you, and shall be in you (John 14:17)

At that day ye shall know that I am in my Father, and ye in me, and I in you (John 14:20)

If ye loved me, ye would rejoice, because I said, I go unto the Father (John 14:28)

. . . he that loveth me shall be loved of my Father, and I will love him, and will manifest myself to him (John 14:21)

. . . and my Father will love him, and we will come unto him, and make our abode with him (John 14: 23)

And . . . the Father . . . shall give you another Comforter, that he may abide with you for ever (John 14:16)

Even the Spirit of truth; whom the world cannot receive (John 14:17)

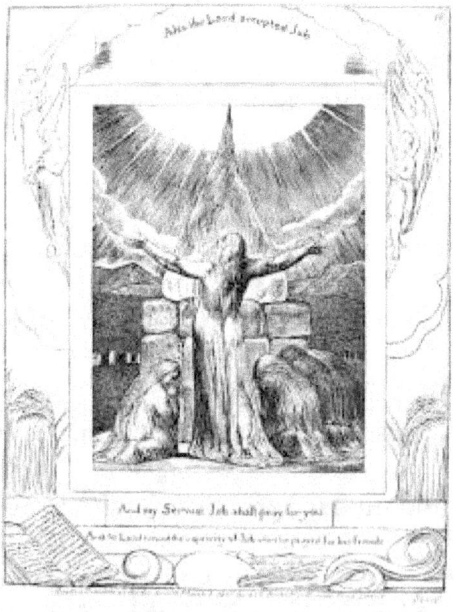

Also the Lord accepted Job

Any my Servant Job shall pray for you

And the Lord turned the captivity of Job when he prayed for his Friends

I say unto you

Love your En-

emies bless then

that curse you

do good to them

that hate you

& pray for them

that despitefull

use you

& persecute you

That you may be

the children of

your Father which

is in heaven, for

he maketh his sun

to shine on the Evil

& on the Good &

sendeth rain on

the Just & the Unjust

Be ye therefore perfect as your Father which is in heaven is perfect

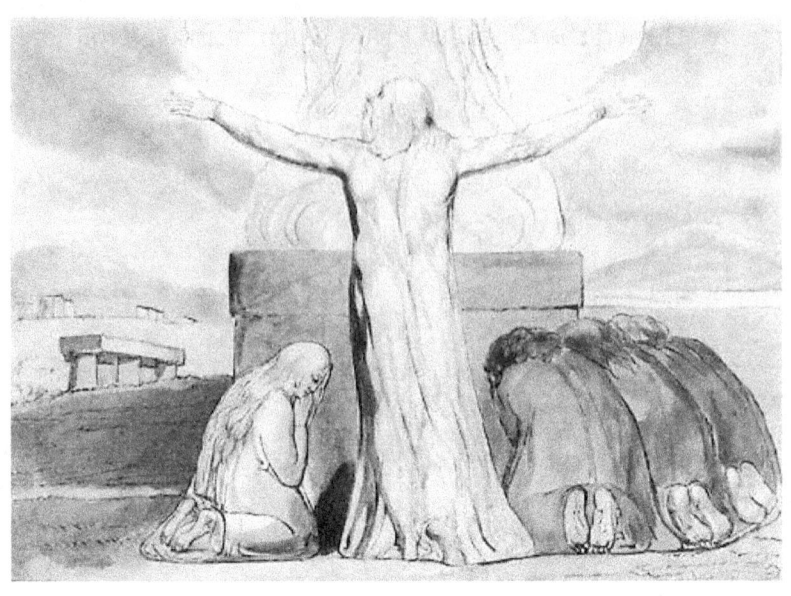

Job's sacrifice

. . . the Lord also accepted Job (Job 42:9)

. . . and my servant Job shall pray for you (Job 42:8)

And the Lord turned the captivity of Job, when he prayed for his friends
(Job 42: 10)

But I say unto you, Love your enemies, bless them at curse you, do good to
them that hate you, and pray for them which despitefully use you, and
persecute you (Matthew 5:45)

That ye may be the children of your Father which is in heaven: for he
maketh his sun to rise on the evil and on the good, and sendeth rain on the
just and on the unjust (Matthew 5: 45)

Be ye therefore perfect, even as your Father which is in heaven is perfect
(Matthew 5: 48)

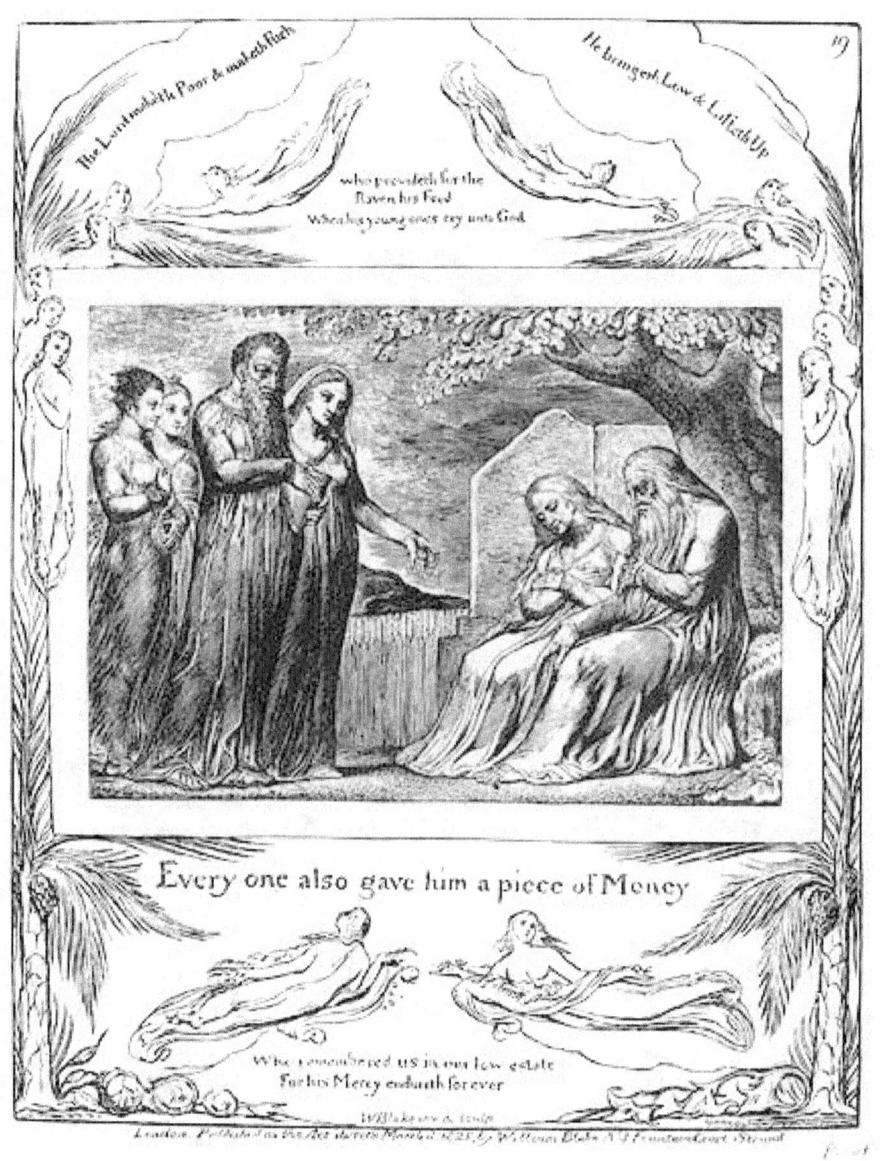

The Lord maketh Poor & maketh Rich

He bringeth Low & Lifteth Up

who provideth for the

Raven his Food

When his young ones cry unto God

Every one also gave him a piece of Money

Who remembered us in our low estate

For his Mercy endureth for ever

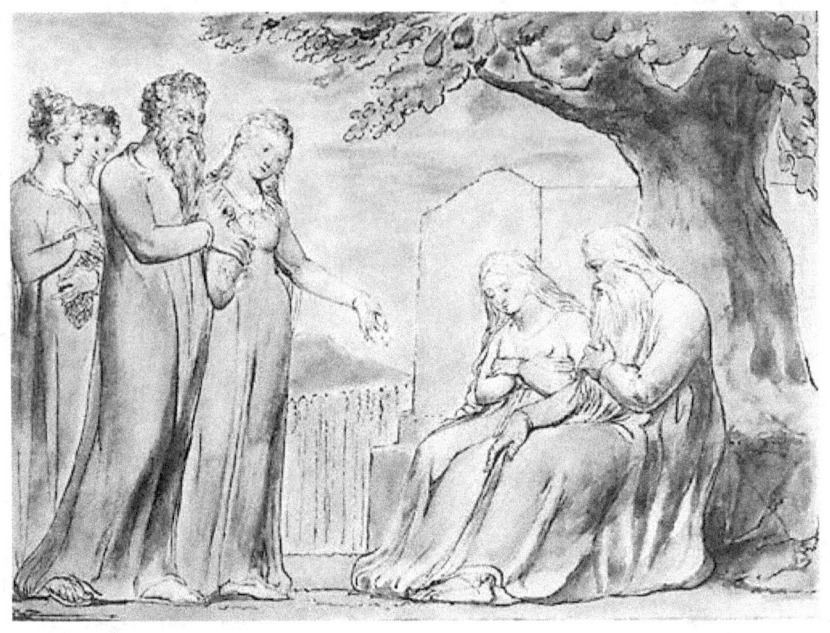

Every man also gave him a piece of money

The lord maketh poor, and maketh rich: he bringeth low, and lifteth up (I Samuel 2:7)

Who provideth for the raven his food? when his young ones cry unto God (Job 38:41)

. . . every man also gave him a piece of money (Job 42: 11)

Who remembered us in our low estate: for his mercy endureth for ever (Psalm 136: 23)

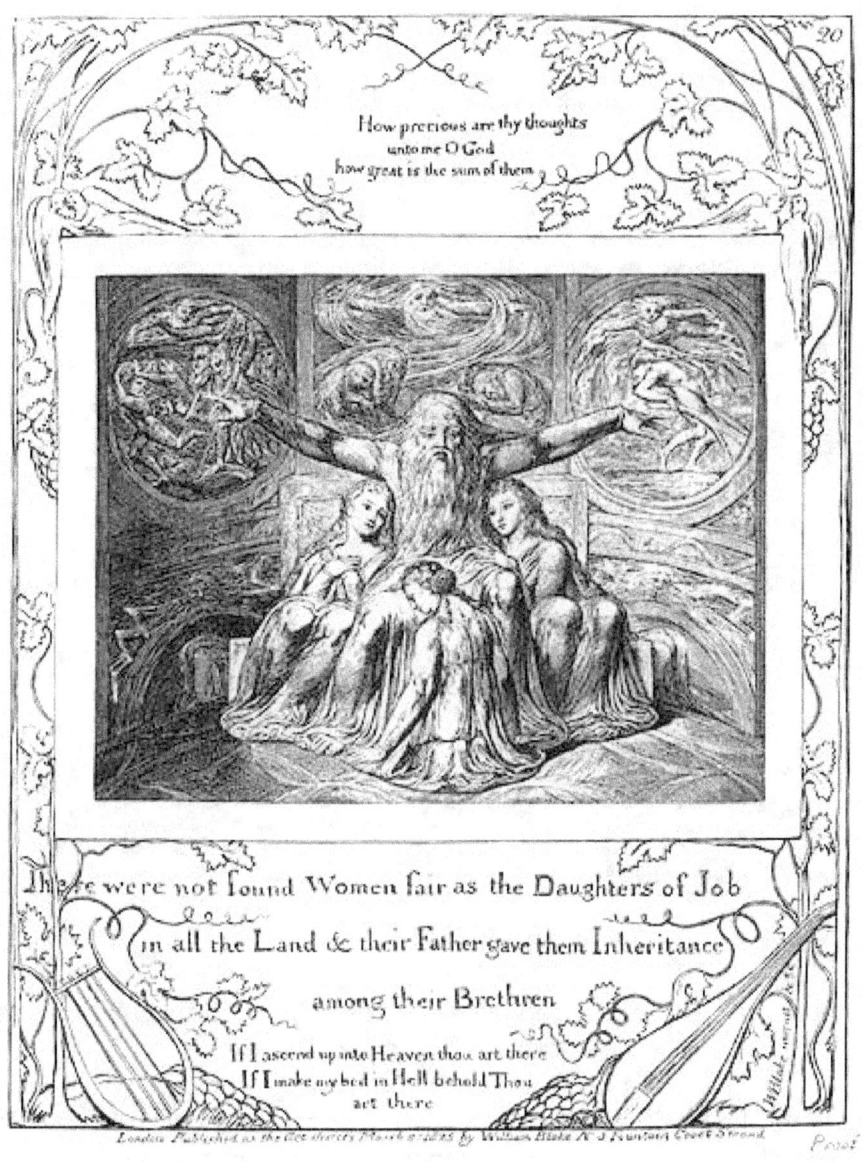

How precious are thy thoughts

unto me O God

how great is the sum of them

There were not found Women fair as the Daughters of Job

in all the Land & their Father gave them Inheritance among their Brethren

If I ascend up into Heaven thou art there

If I make my bed in Hell behold Thou

art there

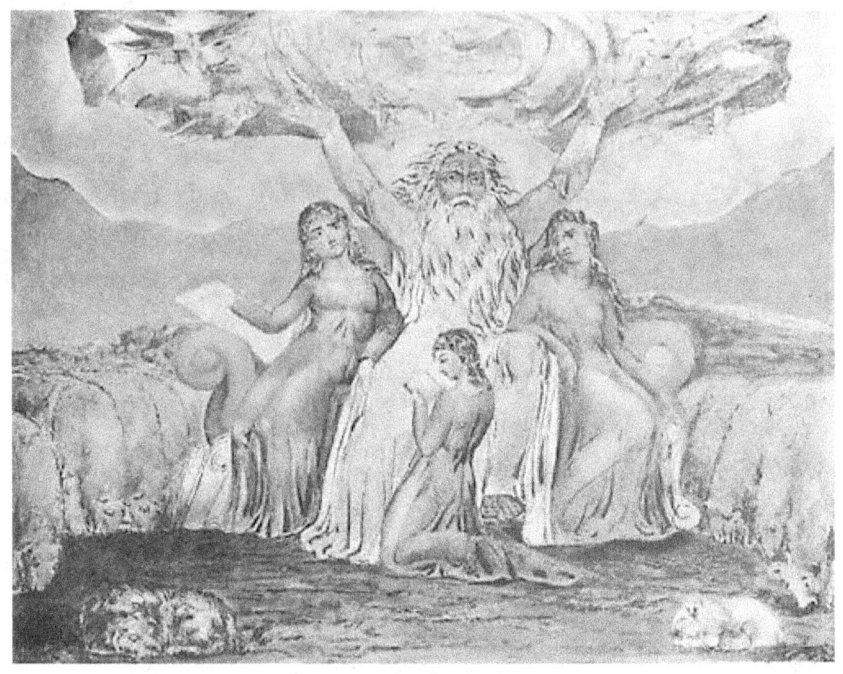

Job and his daughters

How precious also are thy thoughts unto me, O God! how great is the sum
of them! (Psalm 139:17)

And in all the land were no women found so fair as the daughters of Job:
and their father gave them inheritance among their brethren (Job 42:15)

If I ascend up into heaven, thou art there: if I make bed in hell, behold,
thou art there (Psalm 139:8)

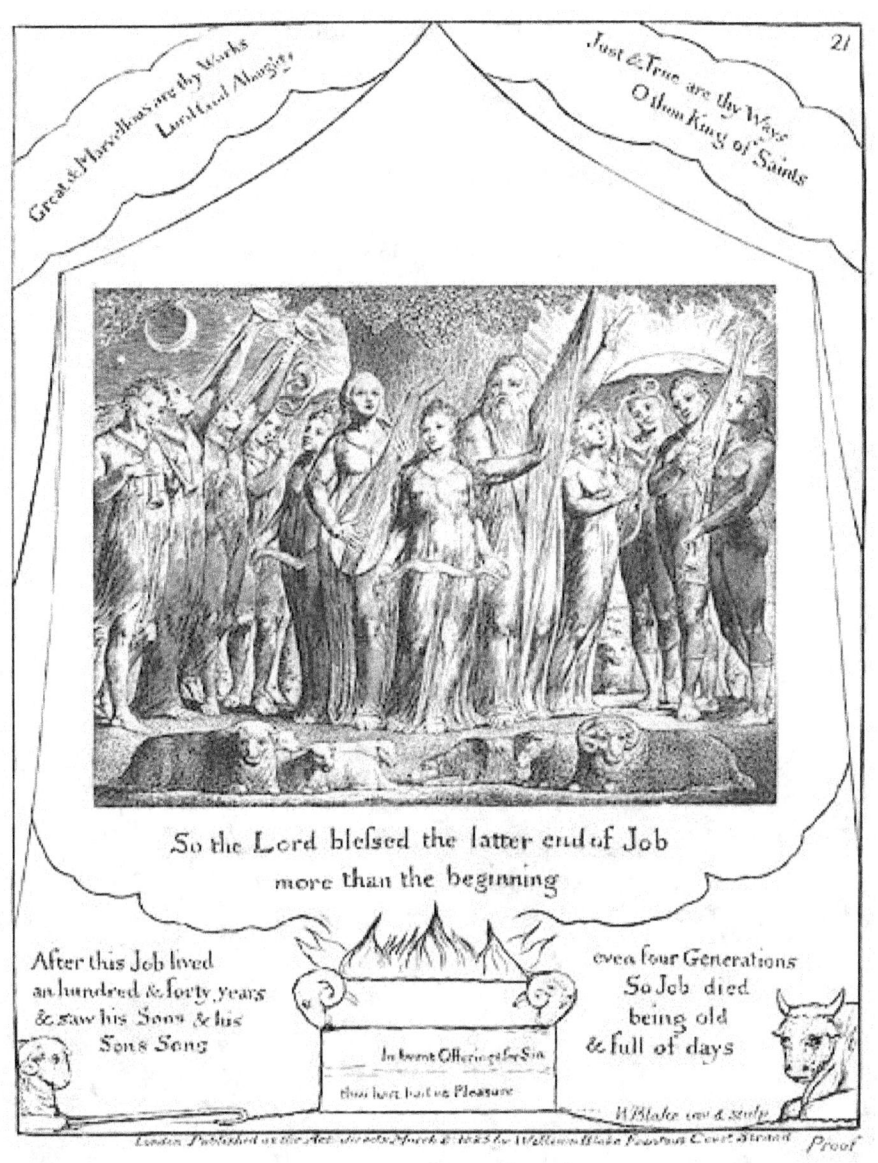

Great & Marvellous are thy Works
Lord God Almighty

Just & True are thy Ways
O thou King of Saints

So the Lord blessed the latter end of Job
more than the beginning

After this Job lived
an hundred & forty years
& saw his Sons & his
Sons Song

even four Generations
So Job died
being old
& full of days

In burnt Offerings for Sin
thou hast had no Pleasure

WBlake inv & sculp

London Published as the Act directs March 8 1825 by William Blake Fountain Court Strand Proof

Great & Marvellous are thy Works

Lord God Almighty

Just & True are thy Ways

O thou King of Saints

So the Lord blessed the latter end of Job

more that the beginning

After this Job lived

an hundred & forty years

& saw his Sons & his

Sons Sons even four generations

So Job died

being old

& full of days

In burnt Offerings for Sin

thou hast had no Pleasure

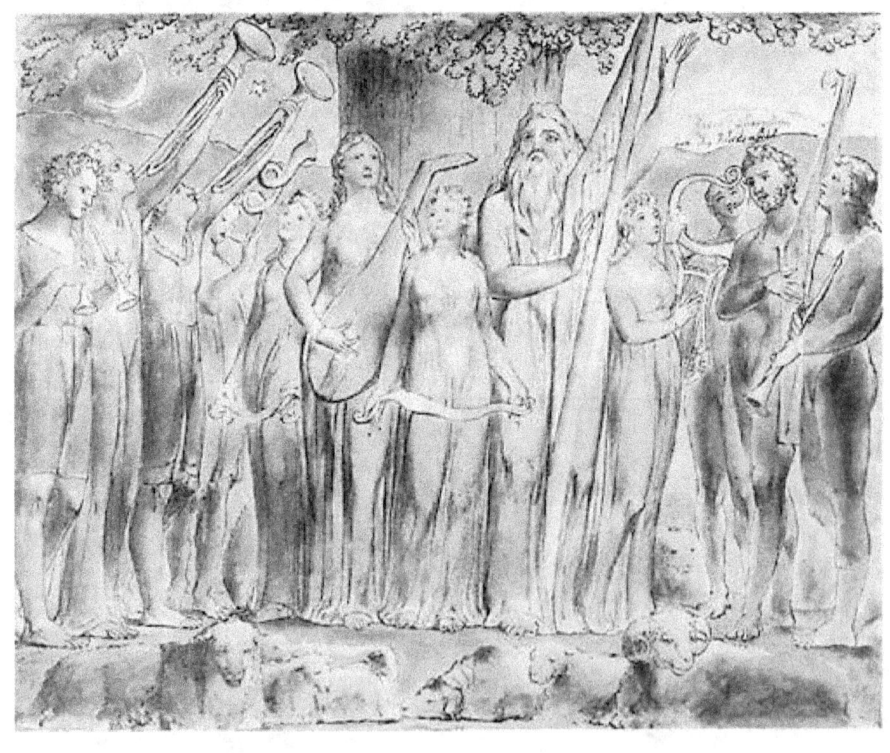

Job and his family restored

Great and marvellous are thy works, Lord God Almighty; just and true are thy ways, thou King of saints (Revelation 15: 3)

So the Lord blessed the latter end of Job more than his beginning (Job 42: 12)

After this lived Job and hundred and forty years, and saw his sons, and his sons' sons, even four generations. So Job died, being old and full of days (Job 42: 16-17)

In burnt offerings and sacrifices for sin thou has had no pleasure (Hebrews 10: 6)

www.ingramcontent.com/pod-product-compliance
Lightning Source LLC
Chambersburg PA
CBHW081638220526
45468CB00009B/2492